PREF

This book would not be possible without the
extensive, unwavering efforts of the clergy and
members of the Nichiren Shu Order of North
America carried out for over 100 years, and
continuing on through to the present. Their efforts
in sharing the Dharma resulted in translation of
materials and the spread of the teachings of
Nichiren Shonin far and wide.

More recently, present day clergy and members
have expanded on the earlier work, resulting in
greater scholarship, more books and articles, and
greater recognition of the Nichiren Shu Order in the
mainstream of Buddhism in the West.

In particular, I offer deep gratitude and appreciation
to my teacher, Ryuoh Faulconer Shonin*, who
guided me on my journey to the priesthood.. I have
advanced because of his guidance and his vision for
the future of our order. While there have been other
teachers along my journey within the Nichiren Shu,
it is this relationship between master and disciple
that has been the foundation. Ryuoh Shonin has also
been instrumental in the growth and development of
the community known today as Myoken-ji Temple.

Ryuoh Shonin has contributed a great deal to our
ability to conduct service in ways more extensive
than can be included here. However, the rendering

i

of the *shōmyo* [Buddhist liturgical chanting/singing] used in this book would not have been possible without his drive, his training, and his vision.

With a deep bow of gratitude and appreciation to all my brothers and sisters in the Dharma,

Myokei Caine-Barrett Shōnin*

[*Shonin is an honorary title used for religious leaders, particularly common in the *Jōdo* and *Nichiren* schools. This title is distinct from that used for Nichiren Shonin and can be observed only through use of the different *kanji* characters.]

INTRODUCTION

This book is intended to provide a guide to daily practice within the Nichiren Shu tradition. The manner of service is the same as that conducted in temples around the world. The practice done by all members and clergy is essentially the same.

The book includes the verse [or Ge] sections of various chapters from the Lotus Sutra, specifically Chapters 2, 3, 10, 11, 12, 16, 21 and 25. Generally speaking, the chapters usually included in a daily service are Chapters 2 and 16, two of the most important chapters of the Lotus Sutra. However, one may choose to combine any of these included portions to accomplish a daily service.

The service can be done fully in *shindoku* [our faith language, a Japanese pronunciation of ancient Chinese], in English, or a mixture of the two. The point is to develop a practice that is both enjoyable and fulfilling.

It should be noted that in Nichiren Shu, percussion is used during service. There are marks to indicate where this begins and ends. The beat is often similar to the beat of one's heart, and can vary based on one's preference. However, our intention is to be reverent and solemn during our practice, and to fully savor the essence of the dharma.

While it is ideal that you develop your practice within a community [sangha], we recognize that it is not possible for everyone. Do your best to honor the Three Treasures [Buddha, Dharma, Sangha] and develop a strong connection to them.

Please enjoy your practice! Should you have any questions or concerns, please feel free send them to nbstx@myoken-ji-usa.org

INDEX

ORDER OF SERVICE

● ● ● *Opening Bell*

DOJO-GE [Practice Hall Verse]   Priest

SANBORAI [Bow to the Three Treasures]   Sangha

● ● ●

KANJO [Invocation]   Sangha

KAIKYOGE [Verses for Opening the Sutra] Sangha

DOKYO [Chanting the Sutra]   Sangha

SOKUN [Nichiren Shonin Instructions] Sangha

SHODAI [Odaimoku Chanting]   Sangha

HOTOGE [Difficulty of Retaining the Sutra] Sangha

EKO [Prayer]   Sangha

SHISEI [Four Great Vows]   Sangha

● ● ●

SANKI [Refuge in the Three Treasures]   Sangha

● ● ●

BUSO [Farewell]   Priest

1

Please make note of the following symbols:

- ●   bell [kanamaru or kanamari]]
- ▲   kei [another bell]
- ■   signal to place hands on book
- ↗   signal to raise book
- ▶   signal for sangha to join in
- »   mokusho [wooden bell]

Pronunciation Guide:

a	ăh
e	ĕh
I	ēē
o	ō
u	ooh

Reads from right to left.

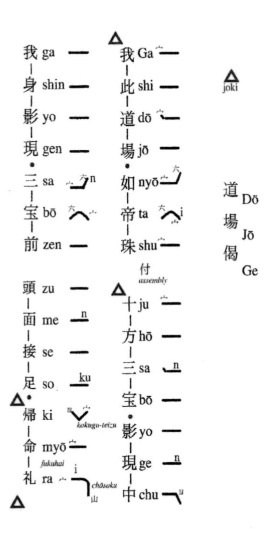

道 Dō
場 Jō
偈 Ge

3

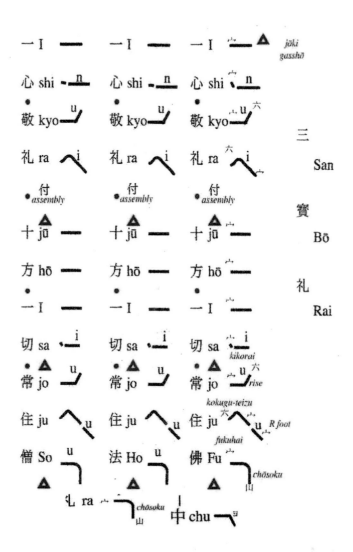

一 I — 一 I — 一 I *jōki gasshō*

心 shi n 心 shi n 心 shi n

敬 kyo u 敬 kyo u 敬 kyo u

礼 ra i 礼 ra i 礼 ra i

付 assembly 付 assembly 付 assembly

十 jū — 十 jū — 十 jū —

方 hō — 方 hō — 方 hō —

一 I — 一 I — 一 I

切 sa i 切 sa i 切 sa i *kikorai*

常 jo u 常 jo u 常 jo u *rise*

住 ju u 住 ju u 住 ju u *kokugu-teizu* R foot

僧 So u 法 Ho u 佛 Fu *fukuhai*

chōsoku

礼 ra *chōsoku* 中 chu

三 San

寶 Bō

礼 Rai

4

Bowing to the Three Treasures

三寳礼

Sanbōrai

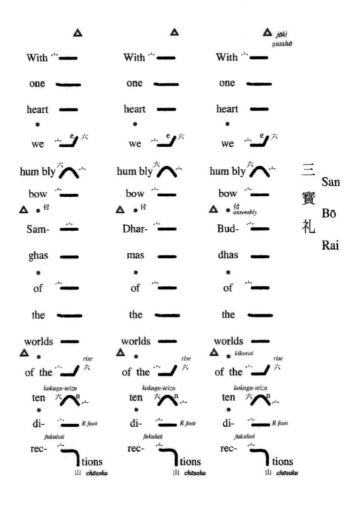

With	With	With — *jōki gasshō*
one	one	one
heart	heart	heart
we	we	we
hum bly	hum bly	hum bly
bow	bow	bow
Sam- · 付	Dhar- · 付	Bud- · 付 *assembly*
ghas	mas	dhas
of	of	of
the	the	the
worlds	worlds	worlds
of the *rise*	of the *rise*	of the · *kikorai* *rise*
kokugu-teizu ten	*kokugu-teizu* ten	*kokugu-teizu* ten
di- *R foot*	di- *R foot*	di- *R foot*
fukuhai rec-	*fukuhai* rec-	*fukuhai* rec-
tions *chōsoku*	tions *chōsoku*	tions *chōsoku*

三寶礼 San Bō Rai

6

Honor be to the Great Mandala,
the perfect circle of all Honorable Ones,
revealed by our founder Nichiren Shonin.

▶ Honor be to the Eternal Buddha Śākyamuni,
our original teacher,
the Lord of the Dharma,
our great Benefactor
who attained enlightenment in the remotest past.

Honor be to the Sutra of the Lotus Flower
of the Wonderful Dharma,
the Teaching of Equality,
the Great Wisdom,
the One Vehicle.

Honor be to our founder,
the Great Bodhisattva Nichiren Shonin,
dispatched by our Original Buddha.

Honor be to Renge-ajari Nichiji Shonin,
the first overseas missionary.

Honor be to the protective deities of the Dharma.
We honor all of you.

May you come to this consecrated place
out of your compassion toward us,
see us with the light of your wisdom
and accept our offering of chanting the Sutra and

Na Mu Myō Hō Ren Ge Kyō

▲▲▲   *KANJO 2*   [Invocation]

Honor be to the Great Mandala of the Most Venerable
One, the Perfect Circle having never been revealed
before in the Age of Degeneration.

▶ Honor be to Śākyamuni Buddha, the Great
Benefactor, the Original Teacher who attained
Buddhahood in the remotest past.

Honor be to Many Treasures Tathagata, who appeared
in this world to bear witness to the Truth of the Sutra
of the Lotus Flower of the Wonderful Dharma.

Honor be to the Buddhas of the worlds of the ten
directions in the past, present and future, the
emanations of the Eternal Śākyamuni Buddha.

Honor be to Jogyo, Anryugyo, Jogyo and Muhengyo,
and the other great bodhisattvas who appeared from
underground, the disciples of the Eternal Śākyamuni
Buddha.

Honor be to Manjushri, Fugen, Maitreya, Yakuo,
Kannon, and the other bodhisattvas, the disciples of
either the historical Śākyamuni Buddha or the Buddhas
who have come from the other worlds.

Honor be to the great beings who appeared as the
disciples of Śākyamuni Buddha and the Tathagatas of

the other worlds: Rahula, Maudgalyayana, Mahakashyapa, Ananda and others. All these great sravakas were newly assured of attaining Buddhahood in the Lotus Sutra.

Honor be to the *shoten zenjin*, who are the heavenly gods and benevolent deities who protect the practitioners of the One Vehicle, especially Myoken Bosatsu, the guardian deity of this temple [may be omitted], Kishimojin, Daikoku-ten, Shichimen, Benzaiten, and Jizo Bosatsu.

We revere all the Three Treasures that abide in the Lotus Sutra. We especially honor our Founder, the Great Bodhisattva Nichiren Shonin, who is the Great Leader of those of us who live in the Declining Latter Age of the Dharma.

Honor be to the Six Major Disciples, the Associated Major Disciples, the Nine Senior Disciples of Nichiro, and the other disciples of Nichiren who have contributed much to our order.

Honor be to Renge-Ajari Nichiji Shonin, the first overseas missionary, and all those who have followed in his footsteps as overseas missionaries.

May all you venerable ones come to this consecrated place out of your compassion toward us, see us with the light of your wisdom, and accept our offering of the savor of the Dharma.

KAIKYOGE
[Verses for Opening the Sutra]

Mujo Jinjin
Mimyo no Ho Wa
Hyakusen Mango nimo
Aitatematsuru
Koto Katashi
Ware Ima Kenmon shi
Juji Surukoto wo Etari
Negawaku wa Nyorai no
Dai Ichigi wo Gesen
▪ Shigoku No Daijo **place hands on sutra*
Shigisu bekarazu
⤴Kenmon Sokuchi **raise sutra to eye level*
Mina Bodai ni Chikazuku
Nosen wa Hoshin
Shosen wa Hosshin
Shikiso no Monji wa
Sunawachi Kore
Ojin nari
Muryo no Kudoku
Mina Kono Kyo ni
Atsumareri
Kono Yueni Jizai ni
Myo ni Kunji
Mitsu ni Yakusu
Uchi Muchi
Tsumi wo Messhi
Zen wo Shozu
Moshi was Shin

Moshi wa Ho
Tomo ni Butsudo wo Jozen
Sanze no Shobutsu   *put sutra down*
Jinjin no Myoden nari
Shojo Sese
Chigu shi Chodaisen
▲

▲ **KAIKYOGE**
[Verses for Opening the Sutra]

The most profound and wonderful teaching
is presented in this sutra.
▶This sutra is difficult to meet even once
in thousands and millions of aeons.
Now we have been able to see, hear, receive and keep
this sutra.
May we understand the most excellent teaching of the
Tathagata!

The most excellent teaching of the Great Vehicle
■is very difficult for us to understand.

**hands on sutra

We shall be able to approach enlightenment
when ↗**we see, hear, or touch this sutra.

***raise
sutra to
eye level*

Expounded is the Buddha's truth   *[Sambhoga-kaya]*
Expounding is the Buddha's essence   *[Dharma-kaya]*
The letters composing this sutra are
the Buddha's manifestation   *[Nirmana-kaya]*

Just as perfume is caught by something put nearby,
so shall we be richly benefitted by this sutra,
even when we are not aware of being so benefitted,
because infinite merits are accumulated in this sutra.

13

We can expiate our past transgressions,
do good deeds,
and attain Buddhahood by the merits of this sutra.

It does not matter whether we are wise or not,
or whether we believe the sutra or slander it.

This sutra is the most wonderful and most excellent
taught by the Buddhas of the past, present, and future.

Put sutra down
May we meet and receive it, birth after birth, world
after world!

MYOHO REN GE KYO HOBEN PON DAI NI
(Chapter II: Expedients)

Ni Ji Se Son
▶ Ju San Mai
» An Jo Ni Ki
Go Shari Hotsu
● Sho But' Chi E
Jin Jin Mu Ryo
Go Chi E Mon
Nan Ge Nan Nyu
● Is' Sai Sho Mon
Hyaku Shi Butsu
Sho Hu No Chi
Sho I Sha Ga
Butsu Zo Shin Gon
Hyaku Sen Man Noku
Mu Shu Sho Butsu
● Jin Gyo Sho Butsu
Mu Ryo Do Ho
Yu Myo Sho Jin
Myo Sho Hu Mon
Jo Ju Jin Jin
Mi Zo U Ho
Zui Gi Sho Setsu
I Shu Nan Ge
Shari Hotsu
Go Ju Jo But' Chi Rai
Shu Ju In Nen
Shu Ju Hi Yu

Ko En Gon Kyo
Mu Shu Ho Ben
In Do Shu Jo
Ryo Ri Sho Jaku
Sho I Sha Ga
Nyo Rai Ho Ben
Chi Ken Hara Mitsu
Kai I Gu Soku
Shari Hotsu
Nyo Rai Chi Ken
Ko Dai Jin Non
Mu Ryo Mu Ge
Riki Mu Sho I
Zen Jo Ge Das'
San Mai
Jin Nyu Mu Sai
Jo Ju Is' sai
Mi Zo U Ho
Shari Hotsu
Nyo Rai No
Shu Ju Hun Betsu
Gyo Ses' Sho Ho
Gon Ji Nyu Nan
Ek' Ka Shu Shin
Shari Hotsu
Shu Yo Gon Shi
Mu Ryo Mu Hen

Mi Zo U Ho
Bus' Shitsu Jo Ju
Shi Shari Hotsu
Hu Shu Bu Setsu
Sho I Sha Ga
Bus' Sho Jo Ju
Dai Ichi Ke U
Nan Ge Shi Ho
Yui Butsu Yo Butsu
Nai No Ku Jin
Sho Ho Jis' So
●Sho I Sho Ho   ***
Nyo Ze So
Nyo Ze Sho
Nyo Ze Tai
Nyo Ze Riki
Nyo Ze Sa
Nyo Ze In
Nyo Ze En
Nyo Ze Ka
Nyo Ze Ho ●
Nyo Ze Hon Matsu Ku Kyo To

*** *This section is repeated three times*

MYOHO RENGE KYO YOKU RYO SHU
Buddha's Wishes for All Beings

[The Coming of the Buddha, Ch II, Expedients]

Kai But' Chi Ken
▶ Shi Toku Sho Jo Ko
» Shutsu Gen No Se
Yoku Ji Shu Jo
● But' Chi Ken Ko
Shutsu Gen No Se
●Yoku Ryo Shu Jo
Go But' Chi Ken Ko
Shutsu Gen No Se
●Yoku Ryo Shu Jo
Nyu But' Chi Ken Do Ko
Shutsu Gen No Se
Shari Hotsu
Ze I Sho Butsu
Yui I Ichi Dai Ji
In Nen Ko
Shutsu Gen No Se.

[The Triple World, Ch. III, A Parable]

San Gai Mu An
Yu Nyo Ka Taku
Shu Ku Ju Man

Jin Ka Hu I
Jo U Sho Ro
Byo Shi U Gen
Nyo Ze To Ka
Shi Nen Hu Soku
Nyo Rai I Ri
San Gai Ka Taku
Jaku Nen Gen Go
An Jo Rin Ya
Kon Shi San Gai
Kai Ze Ga U
Go Chu Shu Jo
Shitsu Ze Go Shi
Ni Kon Shi Sho
Ta Sho Gen Nan
Yui Ga Ichi Nin
No I Ku Go.

[Dispatch of Monks and Nuns, Ch. X, The Teacher of the Dharma]

Ga Ken Ge Shi Shu
Biku Biku Ni
Gis' Sho Shin Ji Nyo
Ku Yo O Hos Shi
In Do Sho Shu Jo

17

Shu Shi Ryo Cho Bo
Nyaku Nin Yok' Ka Aku
To Jo Gyu Ga Shaku
Sok' Ken Hen Ge Nin
I Shi Sa E Go.

*[The Appearance of a Stupa,
Ch. XI, Beholding the
Stupa of Treasures]*

Ni Ji Ho To Chu
Sui Dai On Jo
Tan Gon
Zen Zai Zen Zai
Shaka Muni Se Son
No I Byo Do Dai E
Kyo Bo Sap' Po
Bus' Sho Go Nen
Myo Hok' Ke Kyo
I Dai Shu Setsu
● Nyo Ze Nyo Ze
Shaka Muni Se Son
● Nyo Sho Ses' Sha
Kai Ze Shin Jitsu.

MYO HO REN GE KYO
DAI BA DAT TA HON DAI JU NI
[Chapter XII: Devadatta]

Jin Datsu Zai Huku So
▶ Hen Jo O Jip' Po
» Mi Myo Jo Hos' Shin
Gu So San Ju Ni
●I Hachi Jis' Shu Go
Yu Sho Gon Hos' Shin
Ten Nin Sho Tai Go
Ryu Jin Gen Ku Gyo
●Is' Sai Shu Jo Ryu
Mu Hu Shu Bu Sha
U Mon Jo Bo Dai
Yui But' To Sho Chi
Ga Sen Dai Jo Kyo
Do Dak' Ku Shu Jo
●Ni Ji Shari Hotsu
Go Ryu Nyo Gon
Nyo I Hu Ku
Toku Mu Jo Do
Ze Ji Nan Shin
Sho I Sha Ga
Nyo Shin Ku E
Hi Ze Ho Ki
Un Ga No Toku
Mu Jo Bo Dai
Butsu Do Gen Ko
Kyo Mu Ryo Ko

Gon Gu Shaku Gyo
Gu Shu Sho Do
Nen Go Nai Jo
U Nyo Nin Shin
Yu U Go Sho
Is' Sha Hu Toku
Sa Bon Den No
Ni Sha Tai Shaku
San Ja Ma O
Shi Sha Ten Rin Jo O
Go Sha Bus' Shin
Un Ga Nyo Shin
Soku Toku Jo Butsu
Ni Ji Ryu Nyo
U Ichi Ho Ju
Ke Jiki
San Zen Dai Sen Se Kai
Ji I Jo Butsu
Bus' Soku Ju Shi
Ryu Nyo I
Chi Shaku Bo Satsu
Son Ja Shari Hotsu Gon
Ga Kon Ho Ju
Se Son No Ju
Ze Ji Ship' Pu
To Gon

Jin Shitsu
Nyo Gon
I Nyo Jin Riki
Kan Ga Jo Butsu
Bu Soku O Shi
To Ji Shu E
Kai Ken Ryu Nyo
Kotsu Nen Shi Ken
Hen Jo Nan Shi
Gu Bo Satsu Gyo
Soku O Nan Po
Mu Ku Se Kai
Za Ho Ren Ge
Jo To Sho Gaku
San Ju Ni So
Hachi Jis' Shu Go
Hu I Jip' Po
Is' Sai Shu Jo
En Zetsu Myo Ho
Ni Ji Sha Ba Se Kai
Bo Sas' Sho Mon
Ten Ryu Hachi Bu
Nin Yo Hi Nin
Kai Yo Ken Pi
Ryu Nyo Jo Butsu
Hu I Ji E
Nin Den Sep' Po
Shin Dai Kan Gi
Shit' Cho Kyo Rai
Mu Ryo Shu Jo

Mon Bo Ge Go
Toku Hu Tai Ten
Mu Ryo Shu Jo
Toku Ju Do Ki
Mu Ku Se Kai
Rop' Pen Shin Do
Sha Ba Se Kai
San Zen Shu Jo
Ju Hu Tai Ji
San Zen Shu Jo
Hotsu Bo Dai Shin
Ni Toku Ju Ki
●Chi Shaku Bo Satsu
Gyu Shari Hotsu
Is' Sai Shu E
●Moku Nen Shin Ju

MYŌHŌ RENGE KYŌ
NYORAI JURYO HON DAI JU ROKU

[Chapter XVI: The Duration of the Life of the Tathagata)

Ji Ga Toku Butsu Rai
▶Sho Kyo Sho Kos' Shu
» Mu Ryo Hyaku Sen
Man
Oku Sai A So Gi
●Jo Sep' Po Kyo Ke
Mu Shu Oku Shu Jo
Ryo Nyu O Butsu Do
Ni Rai Mu Ryo Ko
●I Do Shu Jo Ko
Ho Ben Gen Ne Han
Ni Jitsu Fu Metsu Do
Jo Ju Shi Sep' Po
●Ga Jo Ju O Shi
I Sho Jin Zu Riki
Ryo Ten Do Shu Jo
Sui Gon Ni Fu Ken
Shu Ken Ga Metsu Do
Ko Ku Yo Sha Ri
Gen Kai E Ren Bo
Ni Sho Katsu Go Shin
Shu Jo Ki Shin Buku
Shichi Jiki I Nyu Nan
Is' Shin Yoku Ken Butsu
Hu Ji Shaku Shin Myo

Ji Ga Gyu Shu So
Ku Shutsu Ryo Ju Sen
Ga Ji Go Shu Jo
Jo Zai Shi Hu Metsu
I Ho Ben Riki Ko
Gen U Metsu Fu Metsu
Yo Koku U Shu Jo
Ku Gyo Shin Gyo Sha
Ga Bu O Hi Chu
I Setsu Mu Jo Ho
Nyo To Fu Mon Shi
Tan Ni Ga Metsu Do
Ga Ken Sho Shu Jo
Motsu Zai O Ku Kai
Ko Fu I Gen Shin
Ryo Go Sho Katsu Go
In Go Shin Ren Bo
Nai Shutsu I Sep' Po
Jin Zu Riki Nyo Ze
O A So Gi Ko
Jo Zai Ryo Ju Sen
Gyu Yo Sho Ju Sho
Shu Jo Ken Ko Jin
Dai Ka Sho Sho Ji
Ga Shi Do An Non

21

Ten Nin Jo Ju Man
On Rin Sho Do Kaku
Shu Ju Ho Sho Gon
Ho Ju Ta Ke Ka
Shu Jo Sho Yu Raku
Sho Ten Kyaku Ten Ku
Jo Sa Shu Gi Gaku
U Man Da Ra Ke
San Butsu Gyu Dai Shu
Ga Jo Do Hu Ki
Ni Shu Ken Sho Jin
U Hu Sho Ku No
Nyo Ze Shitsu Ju Man
Ze Sho Zai Shu Jo
I Aku Go In Nen
Ka A So Gi Ko
Hu Mon San Bo Myo
Sho U Shu Ku Doku
Nyu Wa Shichi Jiki Sha
Sok' Kai Ken Ga Shin
Zai Shi Ni Sep' Po
Waku Ji I Shi Shu
Setsu Butsu Ju Mu Ryo
Ku Nai Ken Bus' Sha
I Setsu Butsu Nan Chi
Ga Chi Riki Nyo Ze
E Ko Sho Mu Ryo
Ju Myo Mu Shu Ko
Ku Shu Go Sho Toku
Nyo To U Chi Sha

Mot' To Shi Sho Gi
To Dan Ryo Yo Jin
Butsu Go Jip' Pu Ko
Nyo I Zen Ho Ben
I Ji O Shi Ko
Jitsu Zai Ni Gon Shi
Mu No Sek' Ko Mo
Ga Yaku I Se Bu
Ku Sho Ku Gen Sha
I Bon Bu Ten Do
Jitsu Zai Ni Gon Metsu
I Jo Ken Ga Ko
Ni Sho Kyo Shi Shin
Ho Itsu Jaku Go Yoku
Da O Aku Do Chu
Ga Jo Chi Shu Jo
Gyo Do Fu Gyo Do
Zui O Sho Ka Do
I Ses' Shu Ju Ho
●Mai Ji Sa Ze Nen
I Ga Ryo Shu Jo
Toku Nyu Mu Jo Do
●Soku Jo Ju Bus' Shin

MYŌHŌ RENGE KYŌ
NYO RAI JIN RIKI HON DAI NI JU ICHI

[Chapter XXI: The Supernatural Powers of the Tathagatas]

Sho Buk' Ku Se Sha
▶Ju O Dai Jin Zu
» I Es' Shu Jo Ko
Gen Mu Ryo Jin Riki
●Zes' So Shi Bon Den
Shin Po Mu Shu Ko
I Gu Butsu Do Sha
Gen Shi Ke U Ji
●Sho Buk' Kyo Gai Sho
Gyu Tan Ji Shi Sho
Shu Mon Jip' Po Koku
Ji Kai Roku Shu Do
●I Butsu Metsu Do Go
No Ji Ze Kyo Ko
Sho Butsu Kai Kan Gi
Gen Mu Ryo Jin Riki
Zoku Rui Ze Kyo Ko
San Mi Ju Ji Sha
O Mu Ryo Ko Chu
Yu Ko Hu No Jin
Ze Nin Shi Ku Doku
Mu Hen Mu U Gu
Nyo Jip' Po Ko Ku
Hu Ka Toku Hen Zai

No Ji Ze Kyo Sha
Soku I I Ken Ga
Yak' Ken Ta Ho Butsu
Gis' Sho Hun Jin Sha
U Ken Ga Kon Nichi
Kyo Ke Sho Bo Satsu
No Ji Ze Kyo Sha
Ryo Ga Gyu Hun Jin
Metsu Do Ta Ho Butsu
Is' Sai Kai Kan Gi
Jip' Po Gen Zai Butsu
Byo Ka Ko Mi Rai
Yak' Ken Yak' Ku Yo
Yaku Ryo Tok' Kan Gi
Sho Butsu Za Do Jo
Sho Toku Hi Yo Ho
No Ji Ze Kyo Sha
Hu Ku Yaku To Toku
No Ji Ze Kyo Sha
O Sho Ho Shi Gi
Myo Ji Gyu Gon Ji
Gyo Setsu Mu Gu Jin
Nyo Hu O Ku Chu
Is' Sai Mu Sho Ge

O Nyo Rai Metsu Go
Chi Bus' Sho Sek' Kyo
In Nen Gyu Shi Dai
Zui Gi Nyo Jis' Setsu
Nyo Nichi Gak' Ko Myo
No Jo Sho Yu Myo
Shi Nin Gyo Se Ken
No Mes' Shu Jo An
Kyo Mu Ryo Bo Satsu
Hik' Kyo Ju Ichi Jo
Ze Ko U Chi Sha
Mon Shi Ku Doku Ri
●O Ga Metsu Do Go
O Ju Ji Shi Kyo
Ze Nin No Butsu Do
●Ketsu Jo Mu U Gi

MYŌ HŌ REN GE KYŌ
KANZEON BOSATSU HU MON BON
DAI NI JU GO

[Chapter XXV: The Universal Gate
of World-Voice-Perceiver Bodhisattva]

Se Son Myo So Gu
▶Ga Kon Ju Mon Pi
» Bus' Shi Ga In Nen
Myo I Kan Ze On.
●Gu Soku Myo So Son
Ge To Mu Jin Ni
Nyo Cho Kan Non Gyo
Zen No Sho Ho Sho.
●Gu Zei Jin Nyo Kai
Ryak' Ko Hu Shi Gi
Ji Ta Sen Noku Butsu
Hotsu Dai Sho Jo Gan.
●Ga I Nyo Ryaku Setsu
Mon Myo Gik' Ken Shin
Shin Nen Hu Ku Ka
No Mes' Sho U Ku.
Ke Shi Ko Gai I
Sui Raku Dai Ka Kyo
Nen Pi Kan Non Riki
Ka Kyo Hen Jo Chi.
Waku Hyo Ru Ko Kai
Ryu Go Sho Ki Nan

Nen Pi Kan Non Riki
Ha Ro Hu No Motsu.
Waku Zai Shu Mi Bu
I Nin Sho Sui Da
Nen Pi Kan Non Riki
Nyo Nichi Ko Ku Ju.
Waku Hi Aku Nin Chiku
Da Rak' Kon Go Sen
Nen Pi Kan Non Riki
Hu No Son Ichi Mo.
Waku Chi On Zoku Nyo
Kaku Shu To Ka Gai
Nen Pi Kan Non Riki
Gen Sok' Ki Ji Shin.
Waku So O Nan Ku
Rin Gyo Yoku Ju Ju
Nen Pi Kan Non Riki
To Jin Dan Dan Ne.
Waku Shu Kin Ka Sa
Shu Soku Hi Chu Kai
Nen Pi Kan Non Riki

Shaku Nen Toku Ge
Datsu.
Shu So Sho Doku Yaku
Sho Yoku Gai Shin Sha
Nen Pi Kan Non Riki
Gen Jaku O Hon Nin.
Waku Gu Aku Ra Setsu
Doku Ryu Sho Ki To
Nen Pi Kan Non Riki
Ji Ship' Pu Kan Gai.
Nyaku Aku Ju I Nyo
Ri Ge So Ka Hu
Nen Pi Kan Non Riki
Shis' So Mu Hen Bo.
Gan Ja Gyu Huk' Katsu
Ke Doku En Ka Nen
Nen Pi Kan Non Riki
Jin Sho Ji E Ko.
Un Rai Ku Sei Den
Go Baku Ju Dai U
Nen Pi Kan Non Riki
O Ji Toku Sho San.
Shu Jo Hi Kon Yaku
Mu Ryo Ku His' Shin
Kan Non Myo Chi Riki
No Ku Se Ken Ku.
Gu Soku Jin Zu Riki
Ko Shu Chi Ho Ben
Jip' Po Sho Koku Do
Mu Sep' Pu Gen Shin.

Shu Ju Sho Aku Shu
Ji Gok' Ki Chiku Sho
Sho Ro Byo Shi Ku
I Zen Shitsu Ryo Metsu.
Shin Kan Sho Jo Kan
Ko Dai Chi E Kan
Hi Kan Gyu Ji Kan
Jo Gan Jo Sen Go.
Mu Ku Sho Jo Ko
E Nichi Ha Sho An
No Buku Sai Hu Ka
Hu Myo Sho Se Ken.
Hi Tai Kai Rai Shin
Ji I Myo Dai Un
Ju Kan Ro Ho U
Metsu Jo Bon No En.
Jo Sho Kyo Kan Jo
Hu I Gun Jin Chu
Nen Pi Kan Non Riki
Shu On Shit' Tai San.
Myo On Kan Ze On
Bon Non Kai Cho On
Sho Hi Se Ken Non
Ze Ko Shu Jo Nen.
Nen Nen Mos' Sho Gi
Kan Ze On Jo Sho
O Ku No Shi Yaku
No I Sa E Ko.
Gu Is' Sai Ku Doku
Ji Gen Ji Shu Jo

Huku Ju Kai Mu Ryo
Ze Ko O Cho Rai.
Ni Ji Ji Ji Bo Satsu
Soku Ju Za Ki
Ze Byaku Butsu Gon
Se Son
Nyaku U Shu Jo
Mon Ze Kan Ze On
Bo Sap' Pon
Ji Zai Shi Go
Hu Mon Ji Gen
Jin Zu Riki Sha
To Chi Ze nin
Ku Doku Hu Sho
Bus' Setsu Ze Hu Mon
Bon Ji
●Shu Chu Hachi Man
Shi Sen Shu Jo
Kai Hotsu Mu To To
●A Noku Ta Ra San
Myaku San Bo Dai Shin

Myō Hō Ren Ge Kyō
Chapter II: Expedients

There-up-on the World Ho-nored One ▶ E-merged
qui-et-ly » from his Sa-ma-dhi, and said to Sa-ri-pu-
tra:

● "The wis-dom of the pre-sent Bud-dhas is pro-found
and im-meas-ur-a-ble.
The gate to it is dif-fi-cult to un-der-stand and
dif-fi-cult to en-ter.
● Their wis-dom can-not be un-der-stood by any
Sra-va-ka or Prat-ye-ka-bud-dha
be-cause the pre-sent Bud-dhas at-tend-ed on ma-ny
hun-dreds of thou-sands of bil-lions of past Bud-dhas,
● and prac-ticed the in-num-er-a-ble teach-ings of
those Bud-dhas brave-ly and stren-u-ous-ly to their far
flung fame un-til they at-tained the pro-found Dhar-ma
which you have nev-er heard be-fore, and be-came
Bud-dhas, and al-so be-cause since they be-came
Bud-dhas they have been ex-pound-ing the Dhar-ma
ac-cord-ing to the ca-pa-ci-ties of all liv-ing be-ings in
such var-i-ous ways that the true pur-pose of their
var-i-ous teach-ings is dif-fi-cult to un-der-stand.

Sa-ri-pu-tra!
Since I be-came a Bud-dha, I also have been
ex-pound-ing var-i-ous teach-ings with var-i-ous
stor-ies of prev-i-ous lives, with var-i-ous par-a-bles,

and with var-i-ous sim-i-les. I have been lead-ing all liv-ing be-ings with in-nu-mer-a-ble ex-ped-i-ents in order to save them from var-i-ous at-tach-ments, be-cause I have the po-wer to em-ploy ex-ped-i-ents and the po-wer to per-form the par-a-mita of in-sight.

Sar-i-put-ra!
The in-sight of the Ta-tha-ga-tas is wide and deep. The Ta-tha-ga-tas have all the states of mind to-wards in-num-er-a-ble liv-ing be-ings, un-hin-dered el-o-quence,po-wers, fear-less-ness, Dh-ya-na con-cen-tra-tions, e-man-ci-pa-tions, and sa-ma-dhis. They en-tered deep in-to bound-less-ness and at-tained the Dhar-ma which you have nev-er heard be-fore.

Sar-i-pu-tra!
The Ta-tha-ga-tas di-vide the Dhar-ma into var-i-ous teach-ings, and ex-pound those teach-ings to all liv-ing be-ings so skill-fully and with such gen-tle vo-i-ces that liv-ing be-ings are de-light-ed.

Sar-i-put-ra!
In short, the Bud-dhas at-tained the in-num-er-a-ble teach-ings which you have ne-ver heard before. No more, Sar-i-put-ra, Will I say be-cause the Dhar-ma at-tained by the Bud-dhas is the high-est Truth, rare to hear and dif-fi-cult to un-der-stand.

On-ly the Bud-dhas at-tained the high-est Truth,

●that is the re-al-i-ty of all things   ***
in re-gard to their ap-pear-anc-es as such,
their na-tures as such,
their en-ti-ties as such,
their pow-ers as such,
their ac-tiv-i-ties as such,
their pri-mar-y caus-es as such,
their en-vi-ron-men-tal caus-es as such,
their ef-fects as such,
their re-wards and re-tri-bu-tions as such,
●and their e-qual-i-ty as such des-pite these
dif-fer-en-ces.

*** *this section repeats three times*

Myo Ho Ren Ge Kyo Yokuryoshu

Yokuryoshu consists of selected quotes
from the Lotus Sutra

(The Coming of the Buddha) (From Chapter II Expedients)

The Bud-dhas, the World Hon-ored Ones, ▶ ap-pear
in the worlds » in or-der to cause all liv-ing be-ings to
o-pen the gate to the in-sight of the Bud-dha, ●and to
cause them to pu-ri-fy them-selves. They ap-pear in the
worlds in or-der to show the in-sight of the Bud-dha to
all liv-ing be-ings.

● They ap-pear in the worlds in or-der to cause all
liv-ing be-ings to ob-tain the in-sight of the Bud-dha.
●They ap-pear in the worlds in or-der to cause all
liv-ing be-ings to en-ter the Way to the in-sight of the
Bud-dha.

Sa-ri -pu-tra!
This is the one great pur-pose for which the Bud-dhas
ap-pear in the worlds.

(The Triple World) (From Chapter III A Parable)

The tri-ple world is not peace-ful.
It is like the burn-ing house.
It is full of suf-fer-ings.
It is dread-ful.

31

There are al-ways the suf-fer-ings
Of birth, old age, dis-ease and death.
They are like flames
Rag-ing end-less-ly.

I have al-read-y left
The burn-ing house of the tri-ple world.
I am tran-quil and peace-ful
In a bow-er, in a for-est.

This tri-ple world is my prop-er-ty.
All liv-ing be-ings there-in
Are my child-ren.
There are ma-ny suf-fer-ings
In this world.
On-ly I can save
All liv-ing be-ings!

(Dispatch of Monks and Nuns)
(From Chapter X The Teacher of the Dharma)

I will man-i-fest the four kinds of dev-o-tees:
Bhik-sus, bhik-su-nis, and men and wo-men of pure
faith,
And dis-patch them to him
So that they may make of-fer-ings to him,
And that they may lead man-y liv-ing be-ings,
Col-lect-ing them to hear the Dhar-ma from him.

If he is hat-ed and threat-ened
With swords, sticks, ti-le pieces or stones,
I will man-i-fest men and dis-patch them to him
In or-der to pro-tect him.

(The Appearance of a Stupa)
(From Chapter XI Beholding the Stupa of Treasures)

There-up-on a loud voice of praise was heard from
with-in the stu-pa of treas-ures:

"Ex-cel-lent, ex-cel-lent! You, Sak-ya-mu-ni, the
World Hon-ored One, have ex-pound-ed to this great
mul-ti-tude the Su-tra of the Lo-tus Flow-er of the
Won-der-ful Dhar-ma, the Teach-ing of E-qual-i-ty,
the Great Wis-dom, the Dhar-ma for Bo-dhi-satt-vas,
the Dhar-ma up-held by the Bud-dhas.
● So it is, so it is.
What you, Sa-kya-mu-ni,
The World Hon-ored One,
● Have ex-pounded is all true."

MYŌ HŌ REN GE KYŌ
Chapter 12 Devadatta

No soon-er had he said this than the daugh-ter of the drag-on king ▶ came to Sa-kya-mu-ni Bud-dha.'»
She wor-shipped [his feet] with her head, re-tir-ed, stood to one side, and praised him with ga-thas:

● You know the sins and mer-its
Of all liv-ing be-ings.
You il-lum-ine the worlds of the ten quar-ters.
● Your won-der-ful, pure and sa-cred bo-dy
Is a-dorned with the thir-ty-two ma-jor marks
And with the eight-y min-or marks.

● Gods and men are look-ing up at you.
Drag-ons also re-spect you.
None of the liv-ing be-ings
Sees you with-out a-dor-a-tion.

On-ly you know that I am qual-i-fied to at-tain Bo-dhi
Be-cause I heard the Dhar-ma.
I will ex-pound the teach-ings of the Great Ve-hi-cle
And save all liv-ing be-ings from suf-fer-ing.

There-u-pon Sa-ri-pu-tra said to the daugh-ter of the drag-on-king:

"You think that you will be a-ble to at-tain
un-sur-passed en-light-en-ment and be-come a
Bud-dha be-fore long. This is dif-fi-cult to be-lieve
be-cause the bod-y of a wo-man is too de-filed to be a
re-ci-pi-ent of the teach-ings of the Bud-dha. How can
you at-tain un-sur-passed Bod-hi? The en-light-en-
ment of the Bud-dha is far off. It can be at-tained
on-ly by those who per-form the Bod-hi-satt-va
prac-tic-es with stren-u-ous ef-forts for in-num-er-a-ble
kal-pas. A wo-man has five im-poss-i-bil-i-ties. She
can-not be-come the Brah-man Hea-ven-ly-King, King
Sak-ra, King Ma-ra, a wheel-turn-ing-ho-ly-king, and a
Bud-dha. How can it be that you, be-ing a wo-man,
will be-come a Bud-dha,quick-ly or not?"

At that time the daugh-ter of the drag-on-king had a
gem. The gem was worth one thou-sand mil-lion
Su-me-ru-worlds. She of-fered it to the Bud-dha.
The Bud-dha re-ceived it im-med-i-ate-ly. She asked
both Ac-cum-u-lat-ed-Wis-dom Bod-hi-satt-va and
Ven-er-a-ble Sa-ri-pu-tra,"I of-fered a gem to the
World-Ho-nored One. Did he re-ceive it quick-ly or
not?"

Both of them an-swered, "Ve-ry quick-ly."

She said, "Look at me with your su-per-nat-u-ral
pow-ers! I will be-come a Bud-dha more quick-ly."

35

There-u-pon the con-gre-ga-tion saw that the daugh-ter of the drag-on-king changed into a man all of a sud-den, per-formed the Bod-hi-satt-va prac-tic-es, went to the Spot-less World in the south, sat on a jew-elled lo-tus-flower, at-tained per-fect en-light-en-ment, ob-tained the thir-ty-two ma-jor marks and the eight-y mi-nor marks of the Bud-dha, and be-gan to ex-pound the Won-der-ful Dhar-ma to the liv-ing be-ings of the worlds of the ten quar-ters. Hav-ing seen from a-far that the man who had been the daugh-ter of the drag-on-king had be-come a Bud-dha and be-gun to ex-pound the Dhar-ma to the men and gods in his con-gre-ga-tion, all the liv-ing be-ings of the Sa-ha-World, in-clud-ing Bod-hi-satt-vas, Sra-va-kas, gods, drag-ons, the six o-ther kinds, that is, in to-tal eight kinds of su-per-nat-u-ral be-ings, men, and non-hu-man be-ings, bowed to that Bud-dha with great joy. Hav-ing heard the Dhar-ma from that Bud-dha, a group of in-num-er-a-ble liv-ing be-ings of that world un-der-stood the Dhar-ma, and reached the stage of ir-rev-o-ca-bil-i-ty, and a-noth-er group of in-num-er-a-ble liv-ing be-ings of that world ob-tained the as-sur-ance of their fu-ture at-tain-ment of en-light-en-ment. At that time the Spot-less World quaked in the six ways. Three thous-and liv-ing be-ings of the Sa-ha-World reached the stage of ir-rev-o-ca-bil-i-ty, and a-noth-er group of three thou-sand liv-ing be-ings of the Sa-ha-World as-pir-ed for Bod-hi, and ob-tained the as-sur-ance of their

fu-ture at-tain-ment of en-light-en-ment. ● The
Ac-cum-u-lat-ed-Wis-dom Bod-hi-satt-va,
Sa-ri-pu-tra, and all the o-ther liv-ing be-ings in the
con-gre-ga-tion ● re-ceived the Dhar-ma faith-full-y
and in si-lence.

MYŌ HŌ REN GE KYŌ
Chapter XVI The Duration of the Life of the Tathagata

It is man-y hun-dreds of thou-sands
▶ Of bil-lions of tril-lions
» Of a-sam-khyas of kal-pas
Since I be-came the Bud-dha.

● For the past in-nu-mer-a-ble kal-pas
I have al-ways been ex-pound-ing the Dhar-ma
● To man-y hun-dreds of mil-lions of liv-ing be-ings
In or-der to lead them in-to the way to Bud-dha-hood.

● In or-der to save the per-ver-ted peo-ple,
I ex-pe-di-ent-ly show my Nir-va-na to them.
In re-al-i-ty I shall ne-ver pass a-way.
I al-ways live here and ex-pound the Dhar-ma.

Al-though I al-ways live here
With the per-ver-ted peo-ple,
I dis-ap-pear from their eyes
By my su-per-na-tu-ral pow-ers.

When they see me seem-ing-ly pass a-way,
And make of-fer-ings to my sa-ri-ras,
And a-dore me, ad-mi-re me,
And be-come de-vout, up-right and gen-tle,
And wish to see me
With all their hearts
At the cost of their lives,

38

I re-ap-pear on Mt. Sac-red Ea-gle
With my Sam-gha,
And say to them:
"I al-ways live here.
I shall ne-ver be ex-tinct.

I show my ex-tinc-tion to you ex-ped-i-ent-ly
Al-though I nev-er pass a-way.
I al-so ex-pound-ed the un-sur-passed Dhar-ma
To the li-ving be-ings of the oth-er worlds
If they re-spect me, be-lieve me,
And wish to see me.
You have ne-ver heard this;
There-fore, you thought that I pass a-way."

I see the per-ver-ted peo-ple sink-ing
In an o-cean of suf-fer-ing.
There-fore, I dis-ap-pear from their eyes
And cause them to ad-mi-re me.
When they a-dore me,
I ap-pear and ex-pound the Dhar-ma to them.

I can do all this by my su-per-na-tur-al pow-ers.
I live on Mt. Sac-red Ea-gle and
Al-so in the o-ther a-bodes
For a-sam-khya kal-pas.

The per-ver-ted peo-ple think:
"This world is in a great fi-re.
The end of the kal-pa of de-struc-tion is com-ing."
In re-al-i-ty this world of mine is peace-ful.

It is filled with gods and men.
The gar-dens, for-ests, and state-ly build-ings
Are a-dorned with var-i-ous trea-sures:
The je-weled trees have man-y flow-ers and fruits:
The liv-ing be-ings are en-joy-ing them-selves;
And the gods are beat-ing heav-en-ly drums,
Mak-ing var-i-ous kinds of mu-sic,
And rain-ing man-da-ra-va-flo-wers on the great
mul-ti-tude and me.

This pure world of mine is in-de-struct-i-ble.
But the per-ver-ted peo-ple think:
"It is full of sor-row, fear, and o-ther suf-fer-ings.
It will soon burn a-way."

Be-cause of their e-vil kar-mas,
These sin-ful peo-ple will not be a-ble
To hear e-ven the names of the Three Trea-sures
Dur-ing a-sam-khya kal-pas.

To those who have ac-cum-u-la-ted me-rits,
And who are gen-tle and up-right,
And who see me liv-ing here,
Ex-pound-ing the Dhar-ma,
I say: "The du-ra-tion of my life is im-mea-sur-a-ble."
To those who see me af-ter a long time,
I say, "It is dif-fi-cult to see a Bud-dha."

I can do all this by the po-wer of my wis-dom.
The light of my wis-dom knows no bound.
The du-ra-tion of my life is in-num-er-a-ble kal-pas.
I ob-tained this lon-ge-vi-ty by a-ges of prac-ti-ces.

All of you, wise men!
Have no doubts a-bout this!
Re-move your doubts, have no more!
My words are true, not false.

The phy-si-cian, who sent a man ex-ped-i-ent-ly
To tell his per-ver-ted sons
Of the death of their fa-ther in or-der to cure them,
Was not ac-cused of false-hood al-though he was still
a-live.

In the same man-ner, I am the fa-ther of the world.
I am sa-ving all liv-ing be-ings from suf-fer-ing.
Be-cause they are per-ver-ted,
I say that I shall pass away al-though I shall not.
If they al-ways see me,
They will be-come ar-ro-gant and li-cen-tious,
And cling to the five de-si-res
So much that they will fall in-to the e-vil re-gions.

I know who is prac-tic-ing the way and who is not.
There-fore, I ex-pound var-i-ous teach-ings
To all liv-ing be-ings
Ac-cord-ing to their ca-pa-ci-ties.

●I am al-ways think-ing:
"How shall I cause all liv-ing be-ings
To en-ter in-to the un-sur-passed way
●And quick-ly be-come Bud-dhas?"

41

MYŌ HŌ REN GE KYŌ
Chapter 21 The Supernatural Power
of the Tathagatas

The Bud-dhas, the World-Sav-iours, have
Great su-per-nat-u-ral po-wers.
▶ They dis-play their im-meas-ur-a-ble,
su-per-nat-u-ral po-wers
»In or-der to cause all liv-ing be-ings to re-joice.

● The tips of their tongues reach the Heav-en of
Brah-man.
In-num-er-a-ble rays of light are e-mit-ted from their
bod-ies.
● For those who are seek-ing the en-light-en-ment of
the Bud-dha
The Bud-dhas do these things rare-ly to be seen.

● The sound of cough-ing of the Bud-dhas
And the sound of their fin-ger-snap-ping
Re-ver-ber-ate o-ver the worlds of the ten quar-ters,
And the ground of those worlds quakes in the six
ways.

The Bud-dhas joy-full-y dis-play
Their im-meas-ur-a-ble, su-per-nat-u-ral po-wers
Be-cause the Bod-hi-satt-vas from un-der-ground
Vow to keep this su-tra af-ter my ex-tinc-tion.

E-ven if I praise for in-num-er-a-ble kal-pas
The keep-er of this su-tra,
To whom it is to be trans-mitt-ed,

I can-not praise him high-ly e-nough.

His mer-its are as li-mit-less,
As in-fin-ite, as bound-less
As the skies of the worlds
Of the ten quar-ters.

A-ny-one who keeps this su-tra
Will be a-ble to see me.
He al-so will be a-ble to see
Man-y-Treas-ures Bud-dha,
The Bud-dhas of my rep-li-cas,
And the Bod-hi-satt-vas whom I have taught to-day.

A-ny-one who keeps this su-tra will be a-ble to cause
me to re-joice.
He al-so will be a-ble to bring joy
To the Bud-dhas of my re-pli-cas
And al-so to Man-y-Treas-ures Bud-dha who once
passed a-way.

He al-so will be a-ble to see
The pres-ent, past and fu-ture Bud-dhas
Of the worlds of the ten quar-ters
Make of-fer-ings to them, and cause them to re-joice.

The Bud-dhas sat at the place of en-light-en-ment,
And ob-tained the hid-den core.
A-ny-one who keeps this su-tra will be a-ble
To ob-tain the same be-fore long.

A-ny-one who keeps this su-tra
Will be a-ble to ex-pound
The mean-ings of the teach-ings,
And the names and words of this su-tra.
Their e-lo-quence will be as bound-less
And as un-hin-dered as the wind in the sky.

A-ny-one who un-der-stands why the Bud-dhas
ex-pound man-y su-tras,
Who knows the pos-i-tion of this su-tra in the se-ries
of su-tras,
And who ex-pounds it af-ter my ex-tinc-tion
Ac-cord-ing to its true mean-ing,
Will be a-ble to e-lim-i-nate the dark-ness
Of the liv-ing be-ings of the world where he walks
a-bout,
Just as the light of the sun and the moon
E-lim-i-nates all dark-ness,
He will be a-ble to cause in-num-er-a-ble
Bod-hi-satt-vas
To dwell fi-nal-ly in the One Ve-hi-cle.

There-fore, the man of wis-dom
Who hears the be-ne-fits of these mer-its
● And who keeps this su-tra after my ex-tinc-tion,
Will be a-ble to at-tain
● The en-light-en-ment of the Bud-dha
Def-i-nite-ly and doubt-less-ly.

MYŌ HŌ REN GE KYŌ
Chapter 25 Kanzeon Bodhisattva

World-Ho-nored One with the won-der-ful marks!
▶ I ask you a-bout this a-gain.
» Why is the son of the Bud-dha called Kan-ze-on?

●The Ho-nor-a-ble One with the won-der-ful marks
An-swered End-less-In-tent in ga-thas.

Lis-ten! Kan-ze-on prac-tised
Ac-cord-ing to the con-d-i-tions of the plac-es of
sal-va-tion.
●His vow to save peo-ple is as deep as the sea.
You can-not fa-thom it e-ven for kal-pas.

On man-y hun-dreds of thous-ands of mil-lions of
Bud-dhas
●He at-tend-ed and made a great and pure vow.
I will tell you a-bout his vow in brief.
If you hear his name, and see him,
And think of him con-stant-ly,
You will be a-ble to e-lim-i-nate all suf-fer-ings.

Sup-pose you are thrown in-to a large pit of fi-re
By some-one who has an in-ten-tion of kill-ing you.
If you think of the po-wer of Kan-ze-on,
The pit of fi-re will change into a pond of wa-ter.

Sup-pose you are in a ship drift-ing on a great o-cean
Where-drag-ons, fish and de-vils are ram-pant.
If you think of the po-wer of Kan-ze-on,

45

The ship will not be sunk by the waves.

Sup-pose you are pushed
Off the top of Mt. Su-me-ru by some-one.
If you think of the po-wer of Kan-ze-on,
You will be a-ble to stay in the air like the sun.

Sup-pose you are chased by an e-vil man,
And pushed off the top of a moun-tain made of
dia-mond.
If you think of the po-wer of Kan-ze-on
You will not lose e-ven a hair.

Sup-pose band-its are sur-round-ing you,
And at-tempt-ing to kill you with swords.
If you think of the po-wer of Kan-ze-on,
The band-its will be-come com-pass-ion-ate
to-wards you.

Sup-pose you are sen-tenced to death,
And the sword is drawn to be-head you.
If you think of the po-wer of Kan-ze-on,
The sword will sud-den-ly break a-sun-der.

Sup-pose you are bound up
In pill-o-ries, chains, man-a-cles or fet-ters.
If you think of the po-wer of Kan-ze-on,
You will be re-leased from them.

Sup-pose some-one cur-ses you to death,
Or at-tempts to kill you by var-i-ous poi-sons.

If you think of the po-wer of Kan-ze-on,
Death will be brought to that per-son, in-stead.

Sup-pose you meet rak-sa-sas
Or poi-son-ous drag-ons or other de-vils.
If you think of the po-wer of Kan-ze-on,
They will not kill you.

Sup-pose you are sur-round-ed by wild a-ni-mals
Which have sharp, fear-ful tusks and claws.
If you think of the po-wer of Kan-ze-on,
They will flee a-way to dis-tant plac-es.

Sup-pose you meet liz-ards, snakes, vi-pers or
scor-pi-ons
Emit-ting poi-son-ous va-por like flames.
If you think of the po-wer of Kan-ze-on,
They will go a-way as you call his name.'

Sup-pose clouds a-rise, light-ning flash-es,
thun-der peals,
Hail falls, and a heav-y rain comes down.
If you think of the po-wer of Kan-ze-on,
The thun-der-storm will stop at once.

Kan-ze-on will save
All liv-ing be-ings from mis-for-tunes
And from in-num-er-a-ble suf-fer-ings of the world
By the won-der-ful po-wer of his wis-dom.
He has these su-per-nat-u-ral po-wers.
He em-ploys var-i-ous ex-ped-i-ents with his
wis-dom.

In the ten quar-ters there is no k-se-tra
In which he does not ap-pear at all.

Hell, the re-gion of hun-gry spi-rits, and the
re-gion of a-ni-mals,
That is, the three e-vil re-gions will be e-lim-i-nat-ed.
The suf-fer-ings of birth, old age, dis-ease and death
Will grad-u-al-ly be e-lim-i-nat-ed.

He sees the truth of all things and their pur-i-ty.
He sees all things with his great wis-dom.
He sees all things with lov-ing-kind-ness and
com-pas-sion.
Think of him con-stant-ly! Look up at him
con-stant-ly!

All dark-ness is dis-pelled by the light of his wis-dom
As spot-less and as pure as the light of the sun.
The light de-stroys the dan-gers of wind and fi-re,
And il-lu-mines the whole world bright-ly.

His pre-cepts out of his lo-ving-kind-ness brace us up
as thun-der-bolts.
His wish-es out of his com-pas-sion are as won-der-ful
as large clouds.
He pours the rain of the Dhar-ma as sweet as nec-tar,
And ex-tin-guish-es the fi-re of il-lu-sions.

Sup-pose you are in a law-court for a suit,
Or on a bat-tle-field, and are seized with fear.
If you think of the po-wer of Kan-ze-on,
All your e-ne-mies will flee a-way.

His won-der-ful voice comes from his per-ceiv-ing the voice of the world.
It is like the voice of Bra-hman, like the sound of a ti-dal wave.
It ex-cels all the o-ther voi-ces of the world.
There-fore, think of him con-stant-ly!

Do not doubt him e-ven at a mo-ment's thought!
The Pure Saint Kan-ze-on is re-li-a-ble
When you suf-fer, and when you are con-front-ed
With the ca-la-mi-ty of death.

By all these mer-its, he sees
All liv-ing be-ings with his com-pass-ion-ate eyes.
The o-cean of his ac-cum-u-lat-ed mer-its is bound-less.
There-fore, bow be-fore him!' '

There-u-pon Ji-ji Bod-hi-satt-va rose from his seat, pro-ceed-ed to the Bud-dha, and said to him:

"World-Ho-nored One! Those who hear of his su-per-nat-ur-al po-wers by which he o-pened the u-ni-ver-sal gate with-out hin-drance, and which are ex-pound-ed in this chap-ter of Kan-ze-on

Bod-hi-satt-va, know this, will be a-ble to ob-tain not a few mer-its."

● When the Bud-dha ex-pound-ed this Chap-ter of the U-ni-ver-sal Gate, the eight-y-four thou-sand liv-ing be-ings in the con-gre-ga-tion be-gan to a-spi-re

49

● for the un-pa-ra-lleled
A-nut-ta-ra-sam-yak-sam-bod-hi.

RECITATION OF THE ODAIMOKU

NA MU MYŌ HŌ REN GE KYŌ

**Devotion to the
Sutra of the Lotus Flower
of the Wonderful Dharma**

HOTOGE
[Difficulty of Retaining the Sutra]

Shi kyo nan ji

Nyaku zan ji sha

▶Ga soku kan gi

Sho butsu yaku nen

Nyo ze shin nin

Sho butsu sho tan

Ze soku yu myo

Ze soku sho jin

Ze myo ji kai

Gyo zu da sha

So ku i shit' toku

Mu jo butsu do

No o rai se

Doku ji shi kyo

Ze shin bus' shi

Ju jun zen ji

Butsu metsu do go

No ge go gi

Ze sho ten nin

Se ken shi gen

O ku i se

No shu yu setsu

Is' sai ten nin

Kai o ku yo

THE DIFFICULTY OF RETAINING THE SUTRA

It is dif-fi-cult to keep this Su-tra. I shall be glad to see

▶ A-ny-one keep-ing it e-ven for a mo-ment

So will all the o-ther Bud-dhas.

He will be praised by all the Bud-dhas.

He will be a man of va-lor. A man of en-deav-our.

He should be con-sid-ered to have al-read-y

ob-served the pre-cepts, And prac-ticed the dhu-ta.

He will quick-ly at-tain

The un-sur-passed en-light-en-ment of the Bud-dha.

A-ny-one who reads and re-cites this Su-tra in the

fu-ture

Is a true son of mine. He shall be con-sid-ered to live

On the stage of pur-i-ty and good.

A-ny-one, a-fter my ex-tinc-tion,

53

Who un-der-stands the mean-ing of this su-tra,

Will be the eyes of the worlds of gods and men

A-ny-one who ex-pounds this Su-tra

E-ven for a mo-ment in this dread-ful world,

Should be hon-ored with of-fer-ings by all gods

and men.

▲▲▲   *EKO 1*   *[Standard Daily Prayer]*

We respectfully dedicate all our merits now gathered
to the Great Benevolent Teacher,
Śākyamuni the Eternal Buddha;
▶ To the Supreme Teaching, The Lotus Sutra;
To the leader of the Declining Latter Age of the
Dharma,
Our Founder, the Great Bodhisattva Nichiren Shonin;
and to the protective deities of the Dharma.

May all beings under the heavens and within the four
seas live in accordance with the Wonderful Dharma!

May the Wonderful Dharma spread throughout the
Ten Thousand Years of the Declining Latter Age of the
Dharma!

May we realize this world is the Eternal Buddha's Pure
Land!

May peace permeate all the world and all beings enjoy
peace and happiness!

May all beings live in safety and live long without
misfortune!

May the peace and happiness last forever and all
beings be prosperous!

We pray that all beings awaken to the true nature of
reality which is the Buddha Dharma!

May all beings of all realms be helped equally,
overcome suffering,
and gain the happiness of blissful liberation
through the merits of following the teachings of the
Lotus Sutra.

▲   *[additional prayers here if needed]*

We pray for the spirits of our ancestors and for all the
spirits of the universe;

▲   *[additional prayers here if needed]*

May we purify our minds, limit our desires,
learn to be content,
feel free to experience the quiet unassuming joys
of life,
and learn to abandon all attachments formed in the
mind!

With this prayer, we endeavour to increase our
understanding and appreciation
of what others have given and contributed to us
and to develop constant, mindful consideration
of how our thoughts and actions will beneficially
contribute to others.

Na Mu Myō Hō Ren Ge Kyō
▲▲▲

▲▲▲ *EKO 2*   *[Prayer]*

We respectfully dedicate all our merits now gathered
to all the World Honored Ones inscribed on the Great
Mandala,
the Perfect Circle having never been revealed before.
▶ In particular, we honor the Great Bodhisattva
Nichiren,
Our Founder, the Leader of the Declining Latter Age
of the Dharma; and also the ministers who have
contributed so much to our order.
By this, we return the compassionate favor shown to
us.

In addition, we extol the benevolent gods in heaven
and on earth, who protect the Wonderful Dharma.
By this we offer them the enjoyment of the Dharma.

May all beings under the heavens and within the four
seas live in accordance with the Wonderful Dharma!

May the Wonderful Dharma spread throughout the ten
thousand years of the Declining Latter Age of the
Dharma!

May the heavens be boundless and the earth be eternal
and this country be at peace.

May the five kinds of grains be abundant and the
people enjoy their lives.

May the Right Dharma be enhanced and the False Dharma be eliminated.

May peace spread throughout the country by establishing the Right Dharma and the Buddha land be purified and the world be at peace.

May this temple be prosperous and its property safely maintained.

May this temple be protected from fire, burglary, and any other public or private troubles.

May the light of the Dharma burn ever brighter and the soft gentle breeze of this school blow far and wide.

May the temple and its members get along with each other so the Dharma can abide forever.

May the members work hard, comply with the Right Dharma, have safe homes, flourishing families, arouse the mind that aspires to awakening, and maintain the temple.

With this merit, may the overseas ministers who have contributed greatly to the establishment of our order abroad, develop the Way of Perfect Wonder of the Unity of the Three Truths, and may they approach great awakening and purify the Buddha Land. We truly appreciate their virtue and favors.

May all the spirits of the ancestors of the members, especially those spirits who passed away on this particular day [and month if applicable] and the day following this,
the spirits of the newly deceased,
the spirits of those killed by war, sickness, or disasters while serving the public or private good,
and all those in the ocean of the Dharma-realm, whether or not they have formed an affinity with the Buddha Dharma, cut off all confusion and worry, attain awakening, leave suffering behind, and gain joy.

By the power of the Lotus Sutra, may they attain Buddhahood in their present form.

▲   *[Additional prayers here, as needed]*

With additional merit, may we repent of our slander and expiate all other transgressions.

May we strenuously promote the study of the teachings of the Buddha without backsliding.

May we live in safety and live long without misfortune and be loved and respected by all.

May we be able to lead others satisfactorily.

May we be preserved in our right minds at the end of our present lives and confirm the great awakening.

▲   *[Additional prayers here if needed]*

May the merits we have accumulated by this offering be distributed among all living beings, and may we and all other beings attain the awakening of the Buddha.

May all the Dharma Realms equally benefit.

Na Mu Myō Hō Ren Ge Kyō

SHIGUSEIGAN
[The Four Great Vows]

(Shu-jo Mu-hen Se-i-gan-do)
Sentient beings are innumerable:
I vow to save them all.

(Bon-no Mu-shu Se-i-gan-dan)
Our defilements are inexhaustible:
I vow to quench them all.

(Ho-mon Mu-jin Se-i-gan-chi)
The Buddha's teachings are immeasurable:
I vow to know them all.

(Bu-tsu-do Mu-jo Se-i-gan-jo)
The way of the Buddha is unexcelled:
I vow to attain the Path Sublime.

Na Mu Myō Hō Ren Ge Kyō
Na Mu Myō Hō Ren Ge Kyō
Na Mu Myō Hō Ren Ge Kyō

HOTSUGAN
[Four Initiating Vows]

I will cause all living beings to cross the ocean of birth and death if they have not done so.

▶ I will cause them to emancipate themselves from suffering if they have not yet done so.

I will cause them to have peace of mind if they have not yet done so.

I will cause them to attain Nirvana
If they have not yet done so.

Na Mu Myō Hō Ren Ge Kyō
Na Mu Myō Hō Ren Ge Kyō
Na Mu Myō Hō Ren Ge Kyō

FOUR VOWS

I vow to uphold the teaching of
Na Mu Myō Hō Ren Ge Kyō

▶ I vow to practice the teaching of
Na Mu Myō Hō Ren Ge Kyō

I vow to protect the teaching of
Na Mu Myō Hō Ren Ge Kyō

I vow to spread the teaching of
Na Mu Myō Hō Ren Ge Kyō

Na Mu Myō Hō Ren Ge Kyō
Na Mu Myō Hō Ren Ge Kyō
Na Mu Myō Hō Ren Ge Kyō

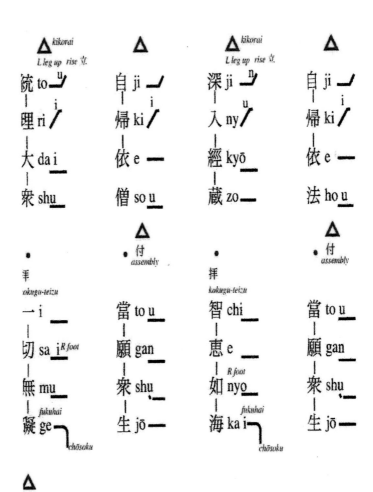

Reads from right to left.

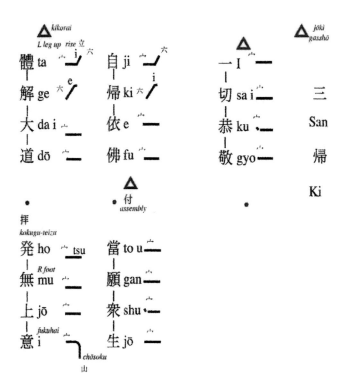

▲ jōki
gasshō

一 I
切 sa i
恭 ku
敬 gyo

三

San

帰

Ki

▲ kikorai
L leg up rise 立
體 ta
解 ge
大 da i
道 dō

自 ji
帰 ki
依 e
佛 fu

▲ 付
assembly

kokugu-teizu
発 ho
無 mu
上 jō
意 i

R foot

fukuhai

chōsoku
山

當 to u
願 gan
衆 shu
生 jō

拝

65

Sanki
Taking Refuge in the Three Treasures

三帰
Sanki

句頭 *kutoshi*

with— re —— vrence, ta–ke ref uge in Bud dha

付 *tsuiteiku*

may all li —— ving be ings

stand

true ly know— the great way

bow   *Rai Hai*

strive for en light en —— ment

句頭 *kutoshi*

Ta —— ke ref —— uge in Dhar ma

may all li——ving be ings

en ter in to su tras

wis dom vast as the———— seas

Ta——ke ref————uge in Sam gha

67

may all li —— ving be ings

cre ate one —— sam gha

with no in ter fear —— ance

*Quote from Chapter 7 of the
Flower Garland Sutra

△ *kikorai*　　　△　　　　　　　　△ *jōki*

true ly 　六 *rise* 立 with

know 　六 the　re-　　vrence

great

way　　　ta ke 　　六

　拝 *kokugu-teizu*　ref uge 六

strive　　　in

for　　　Bud-

en-　　　*R foot*　dha

light- *fukuhai*　△ 付

en-　　ment　may

　山　　　all

chōsoku　　li-　　ving

　　　be-　　ings

三
San

帰
Ki

△	△	△	△
cre ate	ta ke	en ter	ta ke
one	ref uge	in to	ref uge
sam-	in	su-	in
gha	Sam-	tras	Dhar-
• 拜	gha	• 拜	ma
with	△ 付	wis-	△ 付
no	may	dom	may
in-	all	vast	all
ter	li ving	as	li ving
fear-	be- ings	the	be- ings
ance		seas	

R foot

fukuhai

山

chōsoku

70

奉
Bu

送
Sō

71

SOKUN
[Instructions from our founder, Nichiren Shonin]
choose a reading by your preference
or by the date number

1. ▲ *Hokke Shuyō Shō*
[Awakening as Buddha's Children]

We, sentient beings in this *Saha* world, ▶ have all been beloved children of Lord Buddha Śākyamuni since 500 dust-particle *kalpas* ago. Because of our own fault, being undutiful to the Buddha, we have not been aware of being his children until today, but we are not the same as sentient beings in other worlds. The relationship between the Buddha and us, which was established in the remotest past of 500 dust particle *kalpas* ago, is like the moon in the sky reflecting on clear water by itself.
[WNS 2:208]

▲

2. ▲ *Myōhō Ama Gozen Gohenji* [Learn About the Last Moments of Life]

As I contemplate my own life, I, Nichiren, have studied Buddhism ever since I was a child. ▶ One's life is uncertain, as exhaling one's breath one moment does not guarantee drawing it the next; it is as transient as dew before the wind and its end occurs suddenly to everyone, the wise and the ignorant, the aged and the young. I thought I should study the matter first of all before studying anything else.
[WNS 4:141]

▲

72

3. ▲ *Matsuno Dono Gohenji* [Aspiration for Enlightenment]

There are thousands of fish eggs, but few become fish. ▶ Hundreds of mango blossoms bloom, but few become fruit. It is the same with human beings because most people are turned aside by evil distractions. There is an army of warriors wearing armor, but few are able to fight bravely. Many people search for truth, but few attain Buddhahood.

▲

4. ▲ *Sado Gokanki Shō* [Pursuit and Gratitude of Buddhism]

I, Nichiren, vowed to study and master Buddhism ▶ and to attain Buddhahood so that I would be able to save the people from whom I had received favors. To attain Buddhahood, one must not think selfishly even at the cost of his life.

▲

5. ▲ *Shohō Jissō Shō* [Learning and Practice]

Have faith in the Great Mandala Gohonzon, the Most Venerable One in the entire world. ▶ Earnestly endeavour to strengthen your faith, so that you may be blessed with the protective powers of Śākyamuni Buddha, the Buddha of Many Treasures, and Buddhas in manifestation throughout the Universe. Strive to carry out the two ways of practice and learning. Without practice and learning Buddhism will cease to exist. Endeavour yourself and cause others to practice these two ways of practice and learning, which stem from faith. If possible, please spread even a word or a phrase of the sutra to others. [WNS4:79]

▲

6. ▲ *Myōichi Ama Gozen Gohenji*
[Faith and Odaimoku]

Faith is nothing special. ▶ As a wife loves her husband, a husband devotes his life to his wife; as parents do not disown their children, and children do not desert their mother, you should put faith in the *Lotus Sutra*, Śākaymuni Buddha, the Buddha of Many Treasures, all Buddhas throughout the universe, bodhisattvas, and deities. This is faith. [*Nyonin Gosho*, p. 238]

▲

7. ▲ *Zui-ji-I Gosho*
[Merits of the *Lotus Sutra*]

The *Lotus Sutra* is called '*Zui-ji-i*' namely because it expounds the true mind of the Buddha. ▶ Since the Buddha's mind is so great, even if one does not understand the profound meaning of the sutra, one can gain innumerable merits by just reading it. Just as a mugwort among the hemp plants grows straight and a snake in a tube straightens itself, if one becomes friendly with good people, one's mind, behavior and words become naturally gentle. Likewise, the Buddha thinks that those who believe in the *Lotus Sutra* become naturally virtuous. [WNS4:155]

▲

8. ▲ *Kanjin Honzon Shō* [Great Compassion of the Buddha]

When the sky is blue, the land is bright, so those who know the *Lotus Sutra* can see the reasons for occurrences in the world. ▶ For those who are incapable of understanding the truth of the '3,000 existences contained in one thought,' Lord Śākyamuni Buddha, with his great compassion, wraps this jewel with five characters of *myō, hō, re, ge,* and *kyō* and hangs it around the neck of the ignorant in the Latter Age of Degeneration. The four great bodhisattvas will protect such people, just as T'ai-kung-wang and the Duke of Chou assisted the young ruler, King Chen, of the Chou Dynasty, or the Four Elders of the Shang-shan attended child Emperor Hui of the Han Dynasty in ancient China. [WNS2:164]

▲

9. ▲ *Kanjin Honzon Shō* [Keeping the *Odaimoku*]

His, [the Buddha Śākyamuni's], attainment of Buddhahood ▶ are altogether contained in the five words of *myō, hō, ren, ge,* and *kyō* [the *Lotus Sūtra* of the Wonderful Dharma] and that consequently, when we uphold the five words, the merits which he accumulated before and after his attainment of Buddhahood are naturally transferred to us. [WNS2:146]

▲

10. ▲ *Hokke Shoshin Jōbutsu Shō*
[Appearance of Buddha-nature]

A singing bird in a cage attracts uncaged birds, ▶ and the sight of these uncaged birds will make the caged bird want to be free. Likewise, the chanting of *Odaimoku* will bring out the Buddha-nature within ourselves. The Buddha-nature of Bonten and Taishaku will be summoned by the chanting and will protect the chanter. The Buddha-nature of Buddhas and Bodhisattvas will be pleased to be summoned. For attaining Buddhahood quickly, one must lay down the banner of arrogance, cast away the club of prejudice, and chant '*Na Mu Myō Hō Ren Ge Kyō*'

▲

11. ▲ *Myōmitsu Shōnin Goshōku*
[Merits of Chanting *Odaimoku*]

I, Nichiren, sincerely practice the most profound *Lotus Sutra* among all the sutras ▶ which have been preached, are being preached, and will be preached. I also chant *Odaimoku*, the essence of the sutra, by myself and teach others to chant it. The mugwort grass grows straight amidst the hemp field. Trees do not grow straight, but by cutting them straight, they become useful. If you chant the sutra as it states, your mind will be straightened. Be aware that it is hard for us to chant *Odaimoku* unless the spirit of the Eternal Buddha enters into our bodies.

▲

12. ▲ *Shohō Jissō Shō*
[Religious Exaltation]

Tears keep falling when I think of the current unbearable hardships, ▶ but I cannot stop the tears of joy when I think of obtaining Buddhahood in the future. Birds and insects chirp without shedding tears. I, Nichiren, do not cry but tears keep falling. These tears are shed not for worldly matters, but solely for the sake of the *Lotus Sutra*. Therefore, they could be called tears of nectar. [WNS4:79]

▲

13. ▲ *Kaimoku Shō*
[Three Great Vows]

No matter what happens, abandoning the *Lotus Sutra* will cause us to be plunged into hell. ▶ I have made a vow. Even if someone says that he would make me the ruler of Japan on the condition that I give up the *Lotus Sutra* and rely upon the *Kammuryo-ju-kyo [Sutra of Meditation on the Buddha of Infinite Life]* for my salvation in the next life, or even if someone threatens me saying that he will execute my parents if I do not say *Namu Amida-Butsu.* No matter how many great difficulties fall upon me, I will not submit to them until a man of wisdom defeats me by reason. Other difficulties are like dust in the wind. I will never break my vow to become the pillar of Japan, to become the eyes of

Japan, and become the great vessel of Japan. [WNS2:105]

▲

14. ▲ *Itai Dōshin Ji* [One Spirit in Different Bodies]

All things are possible if people are united in one spirit. ▶ Nothing can be accomplished if they are not united. Such teachings also exist in non-Buddhist scriptures. For instance, a king of Yin in old China, King Chieh, who had an army of seven hundred thousand men disunited in spirit, was defeated by King Wu of Chou and his army of eight hundred men, who were united in one spirit. So that if a person has two thoughts, nothing can be accomplished, even if there are hundreds or thousands of people. Yet, if they are united,

they are surely able to accomplish their aim.

▲

15.▲ *Nyosetsu Shugyō Shō* [*Na Mu Myō Hō Ren Ge Kyō* Throughout the World]

When all the people under heaven and the various schools of Buddhism are converted to the One Vehicle teaching, ▶ the *Lotus Sutra*, and when only the *Lotus Sutra* flourishes and all the people recite '*Na Mu Myō Hō Ren Ge Kyō*' in unison, the howling wind will not blow on the branches, falling rain will not erode the soil, and the world will become as ideal as during the reigns of Emperor Fu-hsi and Shen-nung of ancient China. A time is coming when calamities cease to exist, people live long, and people and the land in which they live in become eternal. There should be no doubt about the peaceful

78

life in this world as promised in the *Lotus Sutra*. [WNS4:83]

▲

16.▲ *Risshō Ankoku Ron* [Eternal Truth]

You should promptly discard your false faith and take up the true and sole teaching of the *Lotus Sutra* at once. ▶ Then this triple world of the unenlightened will all become Buddha lands. Will Buddha lands ever decay? All the worlds in the universe will become Pure Lands. Will Pure Lands ever be destroyed? When our country does not decay and the world is not destroyed, our bodies will be safe and our hearts tranquil. Believe these words and revere them! [WNS1:142]

▲

17.▲ *Senji Shō* [Self Respect]

Since I was born ▶ in the land under the Hojo's control, my body appears to follow your order. However, I cannot obey you by heart. [WNS1:243]

▲

18.▲ *Toki Dono Gosho* [Diligent Practice]

Nichiren's followers must strive ▶ to attain Buddhahood by shortening sleeping hours and cutting the time for rest. If not, you will repent forever.

▲

19.▲ *Issho Jobutsu-sho* [On Attaining Buddhahood in this Lifetime]

It also states that, if the minds of living beings are impure, ▶ their land is also impure; but if their minds are pure, so is their land. There are not two lands, pure or impure in themselves. The difference lies solely in the good or evil of our minds.

It is the same with a buddha and an ordinary being. When deluded, one is called an ordinary being; but when awakened, one is called a buddha. This is similar to a tarnished mirror that will shine like a jewel when polished. A mind now clouded by the illusions of the innate darkness of life is like a tarnished mirror; but when polished it becomes like a clear mirror, reflecting the essential nature of phenomena and the true aspect of reality.

Arouse deep faith and diligently polish your mirror day and night. How should you polish it? Only by chanting *Na Mu Myō Hō Ren Ge Kyō* ▲

20. ▲ *Omosu Dono Nyōbō Gohenji* [Buddha and Hell]

First of all, as to the question of where exactly hell and the Buddha exist, ▶ one sutra states that hell exists underground, and another sutra says that the Buddha is in the west. Closer examination, however, reveals that both exist in our five-foot-body. This must be true because hell is in the heart of a person who inwardly despises his father and disregards his mother. It is like the lotus seed which contains both blossom and fruit. In the same way the Buddha dwells within our hearts. For example, flint has the potential to produce fire, and gems have intrinsic value. We ordinary people can see neither our own eyelashes, which are so close, nor the heavens in the distance. Likewise, we do not see that

80

the Buddha exists in our own hearts.

▲

21.▲ *Bō Jikyō Ji*
[Filial Piety]

You [Jōnin Toki] brought your mother's ashes to Minobu and ▶ holding your hands together in *gassho*, you paid homage to the Buddha. You have over-come your sorrow at your mother's death and firmly believed your mother was saved by the teachings of the *Lotus Sutra*. Thus, you were released from your sorrow.

All of your body–your head, hands, legs, and mouth–are inherited from your parents. This kinship between your parents and you is inseparable like the rela-tionship between seed and fruit. Therefore, as your mother is saved, you are also saved by the teachings of the *Lotus Sutra*.
[WNS6:14]

▲

22.▲ *Oto Gozen Goshosoku*
[Letter to Lady Oto]

Ice is made of water, but it is colder than water. Blue colored cloth is colored by indigo, but it will be bluer than indigo when dyed repeatedly. In the same fashion, if you pile up your faith in the *Lotus Sutra*, you will be filled with more vitality and blessings than other people. [*Nyonin Gosho*, p. 124].

▲

23.▲ *Matsuno-dono Nyobo Go-Henji*
[Women's Power]

To put it figuratively, a woman can't feel her pregnancy in the beginning, but after awhile she begins to suspect it ▶ until she knows for sure that she is pregnant. An attentive woman can even tell whether she has conceived a boy or a girl.

The same could be said about the doctrines of the *Lotus Sutra.* If we believe in the merit of *Namu Myoho Renge Kyo*, Śākyamuni Buddha will be conceived in our hearts before we know it, just as a woman is pregnant before she knows it.
[*Nyonin Gosho*, p. 244]
▲

24.▲ *Ji Ri Kuyō Gosho*
[Precious Life]

Fish live in water and water is the treasure to fish; ▶ and trees grow on the land and land is treasure to trees. Likewise, human beings stay alive by feeding themselves with food, so food is their prime treasure. Life is the most precious of all treasures. It is stated in a sutra that nothing in the whole universe is as precious as life and even putting together all the treasures throughout the universe cannot replace life.
[WNS, 4:98]
▲

25.▲ *Kaimoku Shō*
[Showing Gratitude]

To be filial [*kō*] means to be high [*kō*]; ▶ heaven is high but not at all higher than being filial. To be filial [*kō*] also means to be deep [*kō*]; the earth is deep but not any deeper than being filial. Both sages and wise men come from filial devotion. How much more should students of Buddhism realize the favors they receive and repay them? Disciples of the Buddha should not fail to feel grateful for the Four Favors and repay them. [WNS 2:39]

▲

Four Favors = received from parents, all people, sovereign of the nation, and the Three Treasures–Buddha, Dharma, Sangha]

26. ▲ *Kōnichi Bō Gosho*
[Repentance]

As sure as a needle sinks in the water, and rain falls from the sky, a man who kills an ant falls into hell, and a man who cuts off a dead body cannot avoid falling into the three evil regions of hell, hungry spirits, and beasts. Much more so, a man who kills a human. However,

even a large boulder can float with the power of a boat, and a great fire can be extinguished with the power of water. Likewise, if a man does not repent for even a small transgression, he necessarily falls into an evil path, but if a man repents after committing a serious crime, his transgression will be expiated. There are many examples to support this.[WNS5:51]

▲

27. ▲ *Tsuchi-Rō Gosho*
[Practice in Actions, Voice, and Spirit]

Tomorrow, I, Nichiren, will be exiled to Sado Island. ▶ On this cold evening, I am thinking of you in the cold dungeon.

My thought is that you have read and practiced the *Lotus Sutra* with your heart and action, which would save your parents, brothers, sisters, relatives, ancestors, and everyone around you. Other people read the sutra vocally without feeling in their hearts. Even though they might read it with their hearts, they do not experience it as the sutra teaches. Compared to them, you are very precious since you are practicing the sutra in your actions, voice, and spirit. [WNS5:153]

▲

28. ▲ *Myōichi Ama Gozen Goshōsoku*
[Attainment of Buddhahood]

Those who believe in the *Lotus Sutra* are like the winter season for many hardships come incessantly. ▶ Winter is surely followed by spring. We have never heard nor seen that winter returned to fall. We have never heard that the believers in the Lotus Sutra go back to

ordinary men. The *Lotus Sutra* says, 'All people who listen to this sutra will attain Buddhahood.' [WNS7:134]

▲

29. ▲ From the *Senji-Shō*
[Propagation]

Rivers come together to form an ocean. ▶ Particles of dust accumulate to become Mt. Sumeru. When I, Nichiren, began having faith in the *Lotus Sutra*, it was like a drop of water or a particle of dust in Japan. However, when the sutra is chanted a n d transmitted to two, three, ten, a million, and a billion people, it will grow to be a Mt. Sumeru of perfect enlightenment or the great ocean of Nirvana. There is no way other than this to reach Buddhahood. [WNS I:244]

▲

30.▲ *Hō-on Jō*
[Great Compassion]

I, Nichiren, believe my compassion is boundless because I am devoting myself to salvation of all the people, overcoming many persecutions. ▶ Therefore, *Na Mu Myō Hō Ren Ge Kyō*, the teaching for the people in the Age of Degeneration of the Dharma, will spread forever beyond the ten thousand year-period. It has the merit of curing the religious blindness of all people in Japan and blocks the way to hell. This merit is superior to that of Great Masters Dengyō of Japan, T'ien-t'ai of China, Nāgārjuna, of India, and Kāsyapa who was the Buddha's disciple. Therefore, the practice for a hundred years in the peaceful Pure Land is not worth the merit of chanting the *Odaimoku* for one day in this defiled world. Propagation of the *Lotus Sutra* in the two thousand year-period following the death of the Buddha is not worth as much as spreading the *Odaimoku* even a short while in the Age of Degeneration of the Dharma. This is not due to my wisdom; it is solely due to the time of the Age of Degeneration in which I live. [WNS 3:58] ▲

31.▲ *Kanjin Honzon Shō*
[Realization of Buddhahood]

When the Eternal Buddha was revealed in the essential section of the *Lotus Sutra*, ▶ this world of endurance, the *Saha* World, became the Eternal Pure Land, indestructible even by the three calamities of conflagration, flooding, and strong winds, which are said to destroy the world. It transcends the four periods of cosmic change: the *kalpa* of construction, continuance, destruction, and emptiness. Śākyamuni Buddha, the Lord-preacher of this Pure Land, has never died in the past, nor will he be born in the future. He exists forever throughout the past, present, and future. All those who receive his guidance are one with this Eternal Buddha. It is because each of our minds are equipped with the '3,000 modes of existence' and the 'three factors', namely all living beings, the land in which they live, and the five elements of living beings [matter, perception, conception, volition and consciousness]. [WNS 2:148]

▲

Prayer Before Meals

The rays of the sun, moon and stars,
which nurture our spirits,
and the five grains of the earth,
which nourish our bodies,
are all gifts of the Eternal Buddha.
Even a drop of water or a grain of rice
is the result of meritorious work and hard labor.
May this meal help us maintain a healthy body,
mind and spirit
in order to uphold the teachings of the Buddha,
repay the Four Favors,*
and perform the pure conduct of serving others.

Na Mu Myō Hō Ren Ge Kyō

Itadakimasu!

[*The Four Favors:
appreciate the favor received from one's parents;
favor received from one's king (nation);
favor received from all people (community);
favor received from the Three Treasures (Buddha, Dharma, Sangha)]

After Meals

Na Mu Myō Hō Ren Ge Kyō
Na Mu Myō Hō Ren Ge Kyō
Na Mu Myō Hō Ren Ge Kyō

Gochiso sama deshita!

Made in the USA
San Bernardino, CA
01 May 2020